GET YOUR WEBSITE RANKED HIGHER

Simplified Roadmap for Python Programming- Stop Wasting Time and Start Learning the Essentials! What You Need to Know Before You Start Working on Your Website

Stephen Fiordelis

Stephen Fiordelis

Copyright © 2020 Stephen Fiordelis

All rights reserved

The characters and events portrayed in this book are fictitious. Any similarity to real persons, living or dead, is coincidental and not intended by the author.

No part of this book may be reproduced, or stored in a retrieval system, or transmitted in any form or by any means, electronic, mechanical, photocopying, recording, or otherwise, without express written permission of the publisher.

ISBN-13: 9781234567890
ISBN-10: 1477123456

Cover design by: Art Painter
Library of Congress Control Number: 2018675309
Printed in the United States of America

TABLE OF CONTENTS

INTRODUCTION

Python, developed by Guido van Rossum at CWI, has ended up being a commonly utilized general-purpose, top-level program language.

The factor for increasing appeal

- Focus on code readability, much shorter codes, ease of composing
- Developers can reveal rational ideas in fewer lines of code in contrast to languages such as C++ or Java.
- Python supports several shows paradigms, like object-oriented, practical, and vital shows or procedural.
- There exist integrated functions for almost all the often-utilized principles.
- The approach is, "Simplicity is the very best."

LANGUAGE FEATURES

Analyzed

There are no different collection and execution actions, like C and C++.

Straight run the program from the source code.

Internally, Python transforms the source code into an intermediate kind called bytecodes, which is then equated into the native language of a computer system to run it. No requirement to stress over packing and connecting with libraries, and so on.

Platform Independent

Python programs can be established and performed on numerous os platforms.

Python can be utilized on Linux, Windows, Macintosh, Solaris, and a lot more.

Free and Open Source; Redistributable

Top-level Language

In Python, no requirement to make sure about low-level information such as handling the memory utilized by the program.

Simple

Closer to the English language; Easy to Learn

More focus on the option to the issue instead of the syntax

Embeddable

Python can be utilized within the C/C++ program to provide scripting abilities for the program's users.

Robust:

Extraordinary handling functions

Memory management methods in constructed

Rich Library Support

The Python Standard Library has differed largely.

Called the "batteries consisted of" approach of Python; It can assist do different things including routine expressions, document generation, system screening, threading, databases, web internet browsers, CGI, e-mail, XML, HTML, WAV files, cryptography, GUI and a lot more.

The basic library, there are different other premium libraries, such as the Python Imaging Library, which is an exceptionally easy image control library.

WHAT IS PYTHON

Python is an extensively utilized general-purpose, high-level shows language. It was first created by Guido van Rossum in 1991 and established by Python Software Foundation. It was generally established for focus on code readability, and its syntax enables developers to reveal ideas in fewer lines of code.

Python is a programming language that lets you work rapidly and incorporate systems more effectively.

There are 2 significant Python variations-

Python 2 and Python 3. Both are rather various.

Starting with Python shows:

1) Finding an Interpreter:

Prior to we begin Python programs, we require to have an interpreter to analyze and run our programs. There are specific online interpreters like https://ide.pythonforpython.org/, http://ideone.com/, or http://codepad.org/ that can be utilized to begin Python without setting up an interpreter.

Windows: There are lots of interpreters offered easily to run Python scripts like IDLE (Integrated Development Environment) which is set up when you set up the python software application from http://python.org/

Linux: For Linux, Python comes bundled with the Linux.

2) Writing the first program:

Following is the first program in Python

Script Begins

print("python book")

Scripts Ends

Output:

python book

LET US ANALYZE THE SCRIPT LINE BY LINE

Line 1 : [# Script Begins] In Python, remarks start with #. This declaration is for the readability of code and neglected by Python interpreter.

Line 2 : [print("python book")] In a Python script to print something on the console print() function is utilized-- it just prints out a line (and likewise consists of a newline unlike in C). One distinction between Python 2 and Python 3 is the print declaration. In Python 2, the "print" declaration is not a function, and for that reason can be conjured up without a parenthesis.

Line 3: [# Script Ends] This is simply another remark like Line 1.

PYTHON 3 BASICS

Python was established by Guido van Rossum in the early 1990s, and its newest variation is 3.7.1, we can just call it as Python3. Python 3.0 was launched in 2008.

Prior to moving on even more. let's do the most popular 'HelloWorld' custom and thus compare Python's Syntax with C, C ++, Java (I have taken these 3 due to the fact that they are most well-known and primarily utilized languages).

Python code for "Hello World."

nothing else to type

see how simple the syntax is.

print("Hello World")

Keep in mind: Please note that Python for its scope does not depend upon the braces ( ), rather it utilizes imprint for its scope.

Now carrying on additional Let's begin our fundamentals of Python. I will be covering the essentials in some little areas. Simply go through them, and trust me, you'll discover the fundamentals of Python quickly.

INTRODUCTION AND SETUP

If you are on Windows OS, download Python by Clicking here and now set up from the setup and in the start menu type IDLE.IDLE, you can believe it as a Python's IDE to run the Python Scripts.

It   will   look   in   some   way   this:

If you are on Linux/Unix-like, simply open the terminal, and on 99% Linux OS Python comes preinstalled with the OS. Simply type 'python3' in the terminal, and you are ready to go.

It will appear like this:

The " >>> " represents the python shell and its ready to take python commands and code.

Variables and Data Structures

In other program languages like C, C++, and Java, you will require to state the kind of variables; however, in Python, you do not require to do that. Simply key in the variable, and when worth is provided to it, then it will immediately understand whether the worth provided would be an int, float, or char or perhaps a String.

```
# Python program to declare variables
myNumber = 3
print(myNumber)


myNumber2 = 4.5
print(myNumber2)
```

```
myNumber ="helloworld"
print(myNumber)
```

Output:

3

4.5

HelloWorld

See how basic it is, simply develop a variable and appoint it any worth you desire, and after that, utilize the print function to print it. Python has 4 kinds of integrated into Information Structures, specifically Note, Dictionary, Tuple, and Set.

The list is one of the most standard Data Structure in python. The list is a mutable information structure, i.e., products can be contributed to a list later after the list development. It's like you are going to patronize the regional market and made a list of some products, and later you can include a growing number of products to the list.

The append () function is utilized to include information to the list.

```
# Python program to illustrate a list


# Creates A Empty List
Nums = []


# Appending Data in List
Nums.Append(21)
```

Nums.Append(40.5)

Nums.Append("String")

Print(Nums)

Output:

[21, 40.5, String]

Comments:

is used for single-line comment in Python

"This is a comment "is used for multi-line comments

Input and Output

In this area, we will find out how to take input from the user and thus control it or merely show it. input() function is utilized to take input from the user.

Python program to illustrate

getting input from user

name = input("Enter your name: ")

user entered the name 'harssh'

print("hello", name)

Output:

hello harsh

```python
# Python3 program to get input from user

# accepting integer from the user

num1 = int(input("Enter num1: "))

num2 = int(input("Enter num2: "))


num3 = num1 * num2

print("Product is: ", num3)
```

Output:

Enter num1: 8 Enter num2: 6 ('Product is: ', 48)

Selection

Choice in Python is used the two keywords 'if' and 'elif' and else (elseif).

```python
# Python program to illustrate

# selection statement


num1 = 34

if(num1 > 12):

        print("Num1 is good")

elif(num1 > 35):

        print("Num2 is not gooooo....")

else:

        print("Num2 is great")
```

Output:

Num1 is good

Functions

You can consider functions like a lot of code that is planned to do a specific job in the entire Python script. Python utilized the keyword 'def' to specify a function.

Syntax:

def function-name(arguments):

#function body

Python program to illustrate

functions

def hello():

print("hello")

print("hello again")

hello()

calling function

hello()

Output:

hello

hello again

hello

hello again

Now as we understand any program begins with a 'primary' function ... lets produce a primary function like in numerous other programs languages.

```python
# Python program to illustrate

# function with main

def getInteger():

        result = int(input("Enter integer: "))

        return result


def Main():

        print("Started")

# calling the getInteger function and

# storing its returned value in the output variable

        output = getInteger()

        print(output)


# now we are required to tell Python

# for 'Main' function existence

if __name__=="__main__":

        Main()
```

Output:

Started

Enter integer: 5

Iteration (Looping)

As the name recommends, it calls duplicating things again and again. We will utilize the most popular 'for' loop here.

Python program to illustrate

a simple for loop


```
for step in range(5):
        print(step)
```

Output:

0

1

2

3

4

Modules

Python has an abundant module library that has several functions to do numerous jobs. You can find out more about Python's basic library by Clicking here

'import' keyword is utilized to import a specific module into your python code. Think about the following program.

Python program to illustrate

math module

```python
import math

def Main():
    num = float(input("Enter a number: "))
    # fabs is used to get the absolute value of a decimal
    num = math.fabs(num)
    print(num)
if __name__ == "__main__":
    Main()
```

Output:

Enter a number: 85.0

- Crucial distinctions in between Python 2.x and Python 3.x with examples
- Division operator
- print function
- Unicode
- xrange
- Error Handling
- _future_ module

Division operator

If we are porting our code or carrying out the python 3.x code in python 2.x, it can be hazardous if integer department modifications go undetected (because it does not raise any mistake). When porting our code, it is chosen to utilize the drifting worth (like 7.0/ 5 or 7/5.0) to get the predicted outcome.

```python
print 7 / 5
```

```
print -7 / 5
```

Output in Python 2.x

```
1
-2
```

Output in Python 3.x :

```
1.4
-1.4
```

```
# Refer below link for details

#   https://www.pythonforpython.org/division-operator-in-py-
thon/

'''
```

Print Function

This is the most well-recognized modification. In this, the print function in Python 2.x is changed by print() function in Python 3.x, i.e., to print in Python 3.x an additional set of parentheses is needed.

```
print 'Hello, Python'  # Python 3.x doesn't support

print('Hope You like these facts')
```

Output in Python 2.x :

```
Hello, Python

Hope You like these facts
```

Output in Python 3.x :

File "a.py", line 1

    print 'Hello, Python.'

     ^

SyntaxError: invalid syntax

Refer below link for details

https://www.pythonforpython.org/

'''

As we can see, if we utilize parenthesis in python 2.x, then there is no problem; however, if we do not utilize parenthesis in python 3.x, we get SyntaxError.

Unicode:

In Python 2, implicit str type is ASCII. But in Python 3.x implicit str type is Unicode.

print(type('default string'))

print(type(b'string with b '))

Output in Python 2.x (Bytes is same as str)

<type 'str'>

<type 'str'>

Output in Python 3.x (Bytes and str are different)

<class 'str'>

<class 'bytes'>

Python 2.x also supports Unicode

```
print(type('default string '))
print(type(u'string with b '))
```

Output in Python 2.x (Unicode and str are different)

<type 'str'>

<type 'unicode'>

Output in Python 3.x (Unicode and str are same)

<class 'str'>

<class 'str'>

Xrange:

If we require to repeat over the exact same series numerous times, we choose variety() as variety supplies a fixed list. The benefit of xrange() is, it conserves memory when the job is to repeat over a wide variety.

In Python 3.x, the variety function now does what xrange performs in Python 2.x, so to keep our code portable, we may wish to stay with utilizing variety rather. Python 3. x's variety function is xrange from Python 2.x.

```
for x in xrange(1, 5):
        print(x),
```

```
for x in range(1, 5):

        print(x),
```

Output in Python 2.x

1 2 3 4 1 2 3 4

Output in Python 3.x

NameError: name 'xrange' is not defined

Error Handling:

There is a small change in error handling in both variations. In python 3.x, 'as' keyword is needed.

Give it a shot:

```
        trying_to_check_error
except NameError, err:
        print err, 'Error Caused' # Would not work in Python 3.x
```

Output in Python 2.x:

name 'trying_to_check_error' is not defined Error Caused

Output in Python 3.x :

File "a.py", line 3

```
        except NameError, err:

            ^
```

SyntaxError: invalid syntax

'''

```
try:

        trying_to_check_error

except NameError as err: # 'as' is needed in Python 3.x

        print (err, 'Error Caused')
```

'''

Output in Python 2.x:

(NameError("name 'trying_to_check_error' is not defined",), 'Error Caused')

Output in Python 3.x :

name 'trying_to_check_error' is not defined Error Caused

'''

_Future_Module:

This is essentially not a distinction in between 2 variations, however helpful thing to point out here. The concept of __ future __ module is to assist in migration. We can utilize Python 3.x

We can use_future _ imports it in our code if we are preparing Python 3.x assistance in our 2.x code.

In listed below Python 2.x code, we utilize Python 3. x's integer department habits utilizing __ future __ module

```python
# In below python 2.x code, division works
# same as Python 3.x because we use __future__
from __future__ import division

print 7 / 5
print -7 / 5
```

Output :

```
1.4
-1.4
```

Another example where we use brackets in Python 2.x using __future__ module

```python
from __future__ import print_function
print('Pythonforpython')
```

Output :

```
Pythonforpython
```

THE EVOLUTION OF PYTHON LANGUAGE OVER THE YEARS

Python is one of 2015's most common coding languages. Python is also an object-oriented and open source programming language of broad level and general use. In the same period, several developers worldwide have used Python to build GUI apps, websites, and smartphone apps. Python's differentiating feature is that it allows programmers to optimize ideas while creating less readable code. Developers may often use many Python libraries to reduce the time and resources required to develop broad and complex software applications.

A variety of popular websites, including Twitter, Yahoo Groups, Yahoo Charts, Linux Weekly News, Shopzilla, and Online Therapy, currently use the programming language. Python is also very useful in the development of computer, political, scientific and educational applications. Nonetheless, developers also use various language models. According to Python's utilization figures and market share reports from W3techs, Python 2 runs on 99.4% of websites, while Python 3 is used only by 0.6% of websites. Therefore, any programmer needs to learn various versions of Python and its development over several years.

Why has Python developed over the years?

Conceived as a computer hobby initiative

While one of the most common coding languages in 2015, in December 1989, Python was originally developed by Guido van Rossum as a hobby project. While the office of Van Rossum was closing around Thanksgiving, he was searching for a pet project that would hold him occupied over the holidays. He decided to build a modern scripting language interpreter and renamed the idea Python. Python was thus initially developed as an ABC programming language successor. After Van Rossum had written the parser, the text was released in February 1991. Currently, the Python Project Framework operates the open-source programming language.

Version 1 of Python

In January 1994, Python 1.0 was released. A variety of new technologies and practical programming methods, including lambda, filter, chart, and reduce is included in the key paper. Version 1.4 was launched with numerous new features such as keyword claims, enhanced support for complicated numbers, and an integral method of data hiding. Two minor updates, Version 1.5 in December 1997 and Version 1.6 in September 2000, preceded the major releases. Version 1 of Python omitted the functionality of common languages in computing at the period. Nevertheless, the initial prototypes offered a firm base for creating a powerful and modern programming language.

Version 2 of Python

Python 2.0 was published in October 2000 with a modern

list comprehension and garbage collection framework. The list comprehension syntax was influenced by other functional languages such as Haskell. Even Python 2.0 chose alphabetic keywords instead of punctuation symbols, unlike Haskell. The waste management device often produced comparison cycles. Several smaller updates preceded the key edition. Recent updates also introduced several enhancements to the programming language, such as support for nesting scopes and consolidation into one set of Python classes and forms. The Python Framework Base has already announced that no Python 2.8 will exist. Nonetheless, until 2020 the Foundation will support version 2.7 of the programming language.

Version 3 of Python

In December 2008, Python 3.0 was released. This supported several new functionality and enhancements together with some discontinued apps. The reduced functionality and retroactive incompatibility make Python version 3 totally different from previous versions. Most developers still use Python 2.6 or 2.7 to use the capabilities of the last major release. Nevertheless, Python 3's new features make it more modern and common. Some developers have even upgraded to version 3.0 to use these great features.

The incorporated print) (feature has been substituted by Python 3.0, and programmers can use a custom separator between sections. Likewise, the guidelines for order analysis is simplified. If the operators are not arranged in a normal and functional manner, the ordering operators can now increase the exception for TypeError. In comparison to Unicode and 8-bit lines, version 3 of the programming language utilizes text and details instead. This reflects binary data as encoded Unicode when all content is interpreted as Unicode by default.

Because Python 3 is backward inconsistent, programmers cannot use functions such as string exceptions, classes, and associated implied imports. Developers must also be comfortable with syntax and API updates. You can use a "2to3" method to seamlessly shift the code from Python 2 to 3. The platform stresses incompatibility and problems of feedback and alerts. The comments help programmers to update the code and upgrade their existing applications into the new programming language edition.

Latest Versions of Python

Programmers will select either Python edition 3.4.3 or 2.7.10. Python 2.7 helps users to make greater use of numerical processing and upgrades with regular libraries. The update also simplifies the conversion of users to Python 3. Python 3.4, on the other side, arrives with some different library modules and functions, enhancements in protection, and changes in the CPython implementation. Nonetheless, some technologies of the Python API and programming languages are deprecated. The developers will also use Python 3.4 for longer-term support.

Version 4 of Python

Python 4.0 will be accessible in 2023 after Python 3.9 was published. It comes with apps that allow programmers to switch smoothly from version 3 to 4. As they accumulate expertise, Python experts may still use a range of apps that are backward compatible with modernizing their current applications without placing any additional effort and energy. The developers must wait for a good description of Python 4.0, though. However, they need to track the new updates to transition quickly to the common version 4.0 coding language.

Python version 2 and version 3 are entirely different. Any programmer must, therefore, consider the features of these various models and evaluate their capabilities based on project needs. He also must test the Python version provided by each project. However, any developer will use the current Python release to exploit new functionality and long-term support.

KEYWORDS IN PYTHON

Keyword

In programs, a keyword is a "reserved word" by the language which communicates a unique significance to the interpreter. It might be a criterion or a command. Keywords cannot be utilized as a variable name in the program bit.

Keywords in Python: Python language likewise schedules a few of keywords that communicate unique significance. Understanding these is a required part of discovering this language.

Below is a list of keywords signed up by python:

- False, Elif, Lambda,
- None, Else, Nonlocal,
- True, Except, Not,
- And, Finally, Or,
- As, For, Pass,
- Assert, From, Raise,
- Break, Global, Return,
- Class, If, Try,
- Continue, Import, While,
- Def, In, With,
- Del, Is, Yield,

1.True: This keyword is utilized to represent a boolean real. If a declaration holds true, "True" is printed.

2. False: This keyword is utilized to represent a boolean incorrectly. If a declaration is incorrect, "False" is printed.

Real and False in python are like 1 and 0. Example:

Print False == 0

Print True == 1

Print True + True + True

Print True + False + False

3. Note: This is a unique continuous utilized to represent a null worth or space. It's crucial to keep in mind, 0, any empty container(e.g., an empty list) do not calculate to None.

It is a thing of its own datatype-- NoneType. It is not possible to develop numerous None things and can appoint it to variables.

4. And: This a sensible operator in python. "and" Return the very first incorrect value. If not discovered return last. The truth table for "and" is illustrated listed below.

A	B	A and B
True	True	True
True	False	False
False	True	False
False	False	False

3 and 0 returns 0

3 and 10 returns 10

10 or 20 or 30 or 10 or 70 returns 70

5. Or: This a rational operator in python. "or" Return the very first True value if not discovered return last. The truth table for "or" is illustrated listed below.

A	B	A and B
True	True	True
True	False	False
False	True	True
False	False	False

3 or 0 returns 3

3 or 10 returns 3

0 or 0 or 3 or 10 or 0 returns 3

6. Not: This sensible operator inverts the real worth. The truth table for "not" is illustrated listed below.

A	Not A
True	False
False	True

Python code to demonstrate

True, False, None, and, or , not

showing that None is not equal to 0

prints False as its false.

print (None == 0)

showing objective of None

```python
# two None value equated to None

# here x and y both are null

# hence true

x = None

y = None

print (x == y)


# showing logical operation

# or (returns True)

print (True or False)


# showing logical operation

# and (returns False)

print (False and True)


# showing logical operation

# not (returns False)

print (not True)
```

Output:

False

True

True

False

False

Normally utilized to examine the accuracy of the code. If a declaration assessed to real, absolutely nothing occurs, however when it is incorrect, "AssertionError" is raised.

8. Break: "break" is utilized to manage the circulation of the loop. The declaration is utilized to break out of the loop and passes the control to the declaration following right away after the loop.

9. Continue: "continue" is likewise utilized to manage the circulation of code. The keyword avoids the existing model of the loop; however, it does not end the loop.

10. Class: This keyword is utilized to state user-specified classes.

11. Def: This keyword is utilized to state user-specified functions.

12. If: It is a control declaration for decision making. Reality expression forces manage to enter "if" declaration block.

13. Else: It is a control declaration for decision making. Incorrect expression forces manage to enter the "else" declaration block.

14. Elif: It is a control declaration for decision making. It is short for "else if"

15. Del: del is utilized to erase a referral to an item. Any variable or list worth can be erased utilizing del.

```
# Python code to demonstrate

# Del And Assert

# Initializing List

A = [1, 2, 3]


# Printing List Before Deleting Any Value

Print ("The List Before Deleting Any Value")

Print (A)


# Using Del To Delete 2nd Element of List

Del A[1]


# Printing List After Deleting 2nd Element

Print ("The List After Deleting 2nd Element")

Print (A)

# Demonstrating Use of Assert

# Prints Assertionerror

Assert 5 < 3, "5 Is Not Smaller Than 3"
```

Output:

```
The List Before Deleting Any Value

[1, 2, 3]

The List After Deleting 2nd Element

[1, 3]
```

Runtime Error:

Traceback (Most Recent Call Last):

 File "9e957ae60b718765ec2376b8ab4225ab.Py", Line 19, In

 Assert 5 < 3, "5 Is Not Smaller Than 3."

Assertion error: 5 Is Not Smaller Than 3

16. Shot: This keyword is utilized for exception handling, utilized to capture the mistakes in the code utilizing the keyword other than. Code in "attempt" block is examined if there is any kind of mistake, other than a block is performed.

17. Other Than As discussed above, this interacts with "attempt" to capture exceptions.

18. Raise: Also utilized for exception dealing with to clearly raise exceptions.

19. : No matter what is the outcome of the "attempt" block, a block called "lastly" is constantly performed. Comprehensive short article-- Exception Handling in Python

20. For: This keyword is utilized to manage circulation and for looping.

21. While: Has a comparable working like "for," utilized to manage circulation and for looping.

Absolutely nothing occurs when this comes across. This is utilized to avoid indentation mistakes and utilized as a placeholder

23. Import: This declaration is utilized to consist of a specific module into the existing program.

24. From: Generally utilized with import, from is utilized to import specific performance from the module imported.

25. E.g., import mathematics as my math

26. Lambda: This keyword is utilized to make inline returning functions without any declarations enabled internally. In-depth Article-- map, filter, lambda

27. Return: This keyword is utilized to return from the function —comprehensive post-- Return worth in Python.

28. Yield: This keyword is utilized like a return declaration; however, is utilized to return a generator. In-depth Article-- yield keyword

29. With: This keyword is utilized to cover the execution of a block of code within techniques specified by the context manager. This keyword is not utilized much in everyday shows.

30. In: This keyword is utilized to inspect if a container consists of a worth. This keyword is likewise utilized for looping through the container.

31. Is: This keyword is utilized to evaluate things identity, i.e., to inspect if both things take very same memory area or not.

```python
# Python code to demonstrate the working of

# in and is


# using "in" to check

if 's' in 'pythonforpython':

print ("s is part of pythonforpython")

else: print ("s is not part of pythonforpython")


# using "in" to loop through

for i in 'pythonforpython':

        print (i,end=" ")


print ("\r")

# using is to check object identity

# string is immutable(cannot be changed once allotted)

# hence occupy same memory location

print (' ' is ' ')


# using is to check object identity

# dictionary is mutable(can be changed once allotted)

# hence occupy different memory location

print ({} is {})
```

Output:

s is part of python or python

python for python

True

False

32. international: This keyword is utilized to specify a variable inside the function to be of international scope.

33. non-local: This keyword works comparable to the international, however instead of international, this keyword states a variable to indicate variable of outdoors confining function in case of embedded functions.

```
# Python code to demonstrate the working of

# global and non-local


#initializing variable globally

a = 10

# used to read the variable

def read ():

        print (a)


# changing the value of globally defined variable

def mod1():
```

```python
        global a
        a = 5


# changing value of only local variable
def mod2():
        a = 15


# reading initial value of a
# prints 10
read ()


# calling mod 1 function to modify value
# modifies value of global am to 5
mod1()


# reading modified value
# prints 5
read ()


# calling mod 2 function to modify value
# modifies value of local a to 15, doesn't affect global value
mod2()


# reading modified value
```

```python
# again prints 5
read ()


# demonstrating nonlocal
# inner loop changing the value of outer a
# prints 10
print ("Value of a using nonlocal is: ",end="")
def outer ():
        a = 5
        def inner():
        nonlocal a
        a = 10
        inner()
        print (a)

outer()


# demonstrating without nonlocal
# inner loop not changing the value of outer a
# prints 5
print ("Value of a without using nonlocal is: ",end="")
def outer():
        a = 5
        def inner():
```

```
        a = 10

        inner()

        print (a)


outer()
```

Output:

```
10
5
5
```

Value of a using nonlocal is: 10

Value of a without using nonlocal is: 5

PYTHON (VARIABLES, EXPRESSIONS, CONDITIONS, AND FUNCTIONS)

Running your First Code in Python

Now, let us move to compose a python code and running it. Please make sure that python is set up on the system you are working on.

Making a Python file:

Python files are kept with the extension ". Open it and compose the following code:

print "Hello World."

Notice that NO semi-colon is to be used

Checking out the file contents:

Linux System-- Move to the directory site from the terminal where the produced file (hello.py) is kept by utilizing the 'cd' command, and after that type the following in the terminal:

python hello.py

Windows system-- Open command timely and relocate to the directory site where the file is saved by utilizing the 'cd' command and after that run the file by composing the file name as a command.

Variables in Python

Variables require not to be stated initially in python. They can be utilized straight. Variables in python are case delicate as most of the other program languages.

Example: a = 3

A = 4

print a

print A

The output is:

3
4

Expressions in Python

Arithmetic operations in python can be carried out by utilizing math operators and a few of the inbuilt functions.

a = 2

b = 3

c = a + b

```
print c

d = a * b

print d
```

The output is:

```
5
6
```

Conditions in Python

If) declarations, conditional output in python can be gotten by utilizing if-else and elif (else

```
a = 3

b = 9

if b % a == 0:

        print "b is divisible by a"

elif b + 1 == 10:

        print "Increment in b produces 10"

else:

        print "You are in else statement"
```

The output is:

b is divisible by a

Functions in Python

A function in python is stated by the keyword 'def' prior to the name of the function. The return kind of function need not be defined clearly in python. The function can be conjured up by composing the function name, followed by the specification list in the brackets.

Function for checking the divisibility

Notice the indentation after the function declaration

and if and else statements

def check divisibility(a, b):

    if a % b == 0:

    print "a is divisible by b."

    else:

    print "a is not divisible by b"

#Driver program to test the above function

check divisibility(4, 2)

The output is:

a is divisible by b

Python is a really streamlined and less troublesome language to code in. This ease of python is itself promoting its large usage

A statement, Indentation, and Comment in Python

Statements

There are various types of declarations in the Python program language, like Assignment declaration, Conditional declaration, Looping declarations, and so on. N = 50 is a project declaration.

, semi-colon (;-RRB-, extension character slash (\). When the developer requires to do long estimations and cannot fit his declarations into one line, one can make usage of these characters.

Example:

Declared using Continuation Character (\):

```
s = 1 + 2 + 3 + \
    4 + 5 + 6 + \
    7 + 8 + 9
```

Declared using parentheses ():

```
n = (1 * 2 * 3 + 7 + 8 + 9)
```

Declared using square brackets []:

```
footballer = ['MESSI',
        'NEYMAR',
        'SUAREZ']
```

Declared using braces {}:

```
x = {1 + 2 + 3 + 4 + 5 + 6 +
    7 + 8 + 9}
```

Declared using semicolons(;):

```
flag = 2; ropes = 3; pole = 4
```

Indentation

A block is a mix of all these declarations. Block can be concerned as the grouping of declarations for a function.

Among the distinguishing characteristics of Python is its use of imprint to highlight the blocks of code. Whitespace is utilized for imprint in Python.

All declarations with the exact same range to the best come from the very same block of code. If a block must be more deeply embedded, it is just caved in even more to the. You can comprehend it much better by looking at the following lines of code.:

Python program showing

indentation

site = 'gfg'

if site == 'gfg':

        print('Logging on to pythonforpython...')

else:

        print('retype the URL.')

print('All set !')

Output:

Logging on to pythonbook...

All set!

The lines print('Logging on to python or python...') and print('retype the URL.') are two separate code blocks. The two blocks of code in our example if-statement are both indented four spaces. The final print('All set!') is not indented, and so it does not belong to the else block.

j = 1

```
while(j<= 5):

    print(j)

    j = j + 1
```

Output:

1

2

3

4

5

To show a block of code in Python, you should cave in each line of the block by the very same whitespace. The 2 lines of code in the while loop are both indented 4 areas. It is needed to show what block of code a declaration belongs to.

Comments

Python designers frequently make usage of the remark system as, without the usage of it, things can get genuine complicated, genuine quick. Remarks are the beneficial details that the designers offer to make the reader comprehend the source code. Remarks are typically useful to somebody preserving or improving your code when you are no longer around to address concerns about it.

Single line comment: Python single line remark begins with hashtag sign with no white areas (#) and lasts till the end of the line. See the following code bit showing single line comment.:

Code 1:

```
# This is a comment
# Print "Pythonforpython!" to console
print("Pythonforpython")
```

Code 2:

```
a, b = 1, 3 # Declaring two integers
sum = a + b # adding two integers
print(sum) # displaying the output
```

Multi-line string as a comment: Python multi-line remark is a piece of text confined in a delimiter (") on each end of the remark. Once again, there must be no white area in between delimiter (").

When the remark text does not fit into one line, for that reason requires to cover throughout lines, they are beneficial. Multi-line remarks or paragraphs act as documents for others reading your code.

See the following code bit showing multi-line remark:

Code 1:

```
"""
This would be a multiline comment in Python that
spans several lines and describes python or python.
A Computer Science portal for python. It contains
well written, well thought
and well-explained computer science
and programming articles,
```

quizzes, and more.

...
"""

```python
print("Pythonforpython")
```

Code 2:

```python
'''This part on python or python gives you a
perfect example of
multi-line comments'''
print("Pythonforpython")
```

WHY PYTHON IS ESSENTIAL FOR DATA ANALYSIS

Its manufacturers specify the Python language as "... an analyzed, an object-oriented, top-level program language with vibrant semantics. It's top-level integrated information structures, integrated with vibrant typing and vibrant binding, make it really appealing for Fast Application Advancement, in addition to for usage as a scripting or glue language to link existing parts."

Python is a general-purpose program language, indicating it can be utilized in the advancement of both web and desktop applications. It's likewise beneficial in the advancement of intricate numerical and clinical applications. With this sort of flexibility, it comes as not a surprise that Python is among the fastest-growing shows languages on the planet.

How does Python jibe with information analysis? We will be taking a close appearance regarding why this flexible shows language is a need to for anybody who desires a profession in information analysis today or is trying to find some most likely opportunities of upskilling. You'll have a much better concept as to why you ought to pick Python for information analysis as soon as you're done.

What does an information expert do, anyhow? A little refresher on the function of an information expert might assist make it much easier to address the concern about why Python's a great fit. The much better you comprehend a task, the much better options you will make in the tools required to do the task.

Information experts are accountable for translating information and examining the outcomes making use of analytical strategies and offering continuous reports. They establish and execute information analyses, information collection systems, and other methods that enhance analytical effectiveness and quality. They are likewise accountable for obtaining information from secondary or main information sources and keeping databases.

They recognize, examine, and translate patterns or patterns in complicated information sets. Information experts examine computer system reports, hard copies, and efficiency indications to fix and find code issues. By doing this, they can filter and tidy information.

Information experts carry out complete lifecycle analyses to consist of requirements, activities, and style, along with establishing analysis and reporting abilities. They likewise keep track of efficiency, and quality assurance prepares to determine enhancements.

They utilize the outcomes of the above obligations and responsibilities to much better work with management to focus on organization and details requirements.

One requires just to briefly glimpse over this list of data-heavy jobs to see that having a tool that can manage mass amounts of information quickly and rapidly is an outright must. Thinking about the expansion of Big Data (and it's still on the boost), it is essential to be able to manage enormous quantities of details, tidy it up, and procedure it for usage. Python fits the costs because of its simple and ease of carrying out recurring jobs suggest less time requires to be committed to attempting to find out how the tool works.

Data Analysis and Data Science

Prior to pitching in unfathomable on why Python is so vital to information analysis, it's essential initially to develop the relationship between information analysis and information science, given that the latter likewise tends to benefit considerably from the show's language. To put it simply, much of the factors Python works for information science likewise wind up being reasons that it's ideal for information analysis.

The primary distinction in between an information expert and an information researcher is that the previous curate's significant insights from understood information, while the latter offers more with the hypotheticals, the what-ifs. Information experts manage the daily, utilizing information to respond to concerns provided to them, while information researchers attempt to anticipate the future and frame those forecasts in brand-new concerns.

There are typical scenarios where the lines get blurred in between the 2 specialized, which's why the benefits that Python bestows on information science can possibly be the very same ones delighted in by information analysis. Both occupations need an understanding of software application engineering, skilled interaction abilities, standard mathematics understanding, and an understanding of algorithms. Both occupations need an understanding of shows languages such as R, SQL, and, of course, Python.

On the other hand, an information researcher must preferably have strong organization acumen, whereas the information expert does not require to need to fret about mastering that specific skill. Information experts must rather be skilled with spreadsheet tools such as Excel.

As far as wages go, an entry-level information expert can draw in a yearly $60,000 income typically, while the information researcher's typical wage is $122,000 in the United States and Canada, with information science supervisors making $176,000 usually.

So Then, Why Is Python Essential for Data Analysis?

It's Flexible

Then Python is ideal for you if you desire to attempt something innovative that's never ever done prior to; It's perfect for designers who wish to script applications and sites.

It's Easy to Learn

Thanks to Python's focus on simplicity and readability, it boasts a low and progressive knowing curve. Python uses developers the benefit of utilizing fewer lines of code to achieve jobs than one requirement when utilizing older languages.

It's Open Source

Python is open-source, which implies it's totally free and utilizes a community-based design for advancement. There are numerous open-source Python libraries, such as Data adjustment, Data Visualization, Statistics, Mathematics, Machine Learning, and Natural Language Processing, to call simply a couple of (though see listed below for more about this).

It's Well-Supported

Python has a big following and is greatly utilized in commercial and scholastic circles, which suggests that there are plenty of helpful analytics libraries readily available. Python users requiring aid can constantly turn to Stack Overflow, mailing lists, and user-contributed code and paperwork. And the more popular Python ends up being, the more users will contribute details on their user experience, and that indicates more assistance product is readily available at no expense.

To sum up, these points, Python isn't excessively complicated to utilize, the rate is best (totally free!), and there's enough assistance out there to ensure that you will not be given a shrieking stop if a problem occurs. That indicates that this is among those uncommon cases where "you get what you spend for" most definitely does not use!

INPUT/OUTPUT OF PYTHON IN DATA ANALYSIS

Taking input in Python

Designers typically have a requirement to communicate with users, either to get information or to offer some sort of outcome.

Many programs today utilize a dialog box as a method of asking the user to supply input. While Python supplies us with 2 integrated functions to check out the input from the keyboard.

raw_input (prompt)

input (prompt)

Raw Input ( ) : This function operates in older variation (like Python 2. x). That method takes exactly what is entered in the keyboard, converts it into a string, and then returns it to the vector we want to save. For example –

Python program showing

a use of raw_input()

g = raw_input("Enter your name : ")

print g

Output:

Typing of information for the raw_input() function is ended by going into crucial. We can utilize raw_input() to get in numerical information.

Input ( ) : This function very first takes the input from the user and, after that, assesses the expression, which suggests Python instantly determines whether the user went into a number or a string or list.

Then either syntax mistake or exception is raised by python, if the input supplied is not proper. For example –

Python program showing

use of input()

Val = input("Enter your value: ")

print(val)

Output:

How the input function works in Python:

When input() function performs program, circulation will be stopped up until the user has provided an input.

The text or message shown on the output screen to ask a user to go into input worth is optional, i.e., the time will be printed on the screen is optional.

Whatever you get in as input, the input function transforms it into a string., if you get in an integer worth still input() function, transform it into a string. You require to clearly transform it into an integer in your code utilizing typecasting.

Code:

```
# Program to check input
# type in Python

num = input ("Enter number :")
print(num)
name1 = input("Enter name : ")
print(name1)

# Printing type of input value
print ("type of number", type(num))
print ("type of name", type(name1))
output
```

Taking input from console in Python

What is Console in Python? Console (likewise called Shell) is essentially a command-line interpreter that takes input from the user, i.e., one command at a time and translates it.

Then it runs the command and offers necessary output otherwise reveals the mistake message, if it is mistake totally free. A Python Console appears like this.

Here we compose command, and to perform the command, simply press enter key, and your command will be translated.

For coding in Python, you should understand the fundamentals of the console utilized in Python

The main timely of the python console is the 3 greater than signs

```
>>>
```

When after carrying out the very first command, these triggers have appeared, you are complimentary to compose the next command on the shell just. The Python Console accepts command in Python, which you compose after the timely.

Accepting Input from Console

The user goes into the worths in the Console, which is worth then utilized in the program as it was needed.

To take input from the user we use an integrated function input().

```
# input

input1 = input()

# output

print(input1)
```

We can likewise typecast this input to integer, float, or string by defining the input() function inside the type.

Typecasting the input to Integer: There might be conditions when you may need integer input from user/Console, the following code takes 2 input(integer/float) from console and typecasts them to integer then prints the amount.

```
# input

num1 = int(input())

num2 = int(input())
```

```
# printing the sum in integer

print(num1 + num2)
```

Typecasting the input to Float: To convert the input to float the following code will work out.

```
# input

num1 = float(input())

num2 = float(input())


# printing the sum in float

print(num1 + num2)
```

Typecasting the input to String: All sorts of input can be transformed into string type, whether they are float or integer. We utilize keyword str for typecasting.

```
# input

string = str(input())


# output

print(string)
```

Taking multiple inputs from the user in Python

Designer frequently desires a user to get in several worths or inputs in one line. In C++/ C, users can take several inputs in one line utilizing scanf; however, in Python, users can take numerous worths or inputs in one line by 2 approaches.

- Using split() method
- Using List comprehension

Using split() method:

It breaks the provided input by the defined separator. If the separator is not offered, then any white area is a separator.

Syntax:

input().split(separator, maxsplit)

Example:

```
# Python program showing how to

# multiple input using split

# taking two inputs at a time

x, y = input("Enter a two value: ").split()

print("Number of boys: ", x)

print("Number of girls: ", y)

print()


# taking three inputs at a time

x, y, z = input("Enter a three value: ").split()

print("Total number of students: ", x)

print("Number of boys is : ", y)

print("Number of girls is : ", z)
```

```python
print()

# taking two inputs at a time
a, b = input("Enter a two value: ").split()
print("First number is {} and second number is {}".format(a, b))
print()
# taking multiple inputs at a time
# and type casting using list() function
x = list(map(int, input("Enter a multiple value: ").split()))
print("List of students: ", x)
```

Output:

Using List comprehension:

List understanding is a sophisticated method to develop and specify list in Python. We can produce lists much like mathematical statements in one line just. It is likewise utilized in getting several inputs from a user.

Example:

```python
# Python program showing
# how to take multiple input
# using List comprehension

# taking two input at a time
x, y = [int(x) for x in input("Enter two value: ").split()]
```

```python
print("First Number is: ", x)

print("Second Number is: ", y)

print()


# taking three input at a time

x, y, z = [int(x) for x in input("Enter three value: ").split()]

print("First Number is: ", x)

print("Second Number is: ", y)

print("Third Number is: ", z)

print()


# taking two inputs at a time

x, y = [int(x) for x in input("Enter two value: ").split()]

print("First number is {} and second number is {}".format(x, y))

print()


# taking multiple inputs at a time

x = [int(x) for x in input("Enter multiple value: ").split()]

print("Number of list is: ", x)

output
```

Vulnerability in input() function – Python 2.x

This area focuses on checking out the vulnerability and discussing in the input() function in Python 2.x. In Python 3, the raw_input() function was eliminated, and its performance was moved to a brand-new integrated function referred to as input().

Ways to input data in Python 2.x

There are two common methods to receive input in Python 2.x:

Utilizing the input() function: This function takes the worth and kind of the input you get in as it lacks customizing any type.

Utilizing the raw_input() function: This function clearly transforms the input you offer to type string,

Let us utilize the following program to identify the distinction between the two:

Python 2.x program to show differences between

input() and raw input()function

3 inputs using raw_input() function,

after which data type of the value

entered is displayed

s1 = raw_input("Enter input to test raw_input() function: ")

print type(s1)

s2 = raw_input("Enter input to test raw_input() function: ")

print type(s2)

s3 = raw_input("Enter input to test raw_input() function: ")

print type(s3)

3 inputs using input() function,

```python
# after which data type of the value
# entered is displayed
s4 = input("Enter input to test input() function: ")
print type(s4)


s5 = input("Enter input to test input() function: ")
print type(s5)


s6 = input("Enter input to test input() function: ")
print type(s6)
```

Input:

Hello

456

[1,2,3]

45
"goodbye"

[1,2,3]

Output:

Enter input to test raw_input() function: <type 'str'>

Enter input to test raw_input() function: <type 'str'>

Enter input to test raw_input() function: <type 'str'>

Enter input to test input() function: <type 'int'>

Enter input to test input() function: <type 'str'>

Enter input to test input() function: <type 'list'>

Keep in mind: While providing string input in the input() function, we need to confine it to worth in double-quotes. This is not needed in raw_input().

Vulnerability in input() method

The vulnerability in input() technique depends on the truth that the variable accessing the worth of input can be accessed by anybody simply by utilizing the name of variable or approach. Let's check out these ones by one:

Variable name as input specification: The variable having the worth of input variable could access the worth of the input variable straight.

Python 2.x program to show Vulnerabilities

in input() function using a variable

Import Random

Secret_Number = Random.Randint (1,500)

print "Pick a number between 1 to 500"

while True:

    res = input("Guess the number: ")

    if res==secret_number:

    print "You win"

    break

```
        else:

        print "You lose"

        continue
```

Input:

15
Output:

Pick a number between 1 to 500

Guess the number: You lose

Guess the number:

Input:

secret_number

Output:

Pick a number between 1 to 500

Guess the number: You win

As can be seen, in 2nd case, the variable "secret_number" can be straight offered as input, and response is constantly "You won." It examines the variable as if a number was straight gotten in, which indicates it returns a True Boolean constantly. It would not be necessary to use raw input because the attribute cannot be tested straight.

Function name as a criterion: The vulnerability lies here as we can even offer the name of a function as input and gain access to worths that are otherwise not suggested to be accessed.

Python 2.x program to demonstrate input() function

```python
# vulnerability bypassing function name as parameter
secret_value = 500


# function that returns the secret value
def secretfunction():
        return secret_value


# using raw_input() to enter the number
input1 = raw_input("Raw_input(): Guess secret number: ")


# input1 will be explicitly converted to a string
if input1 == secret_value:
        print "You guessed correct"
else:
        print "wrong answer"
# using input() to enter the number
input2 = input("Input(): Guess the secret number: ")


#input2 is evaluated as it is entered
if input2 == secret_value:
        print "You guessed correct"
else:
        print "wrong answer"
```

Input:

400

secret function()

Output:

Raw_input(): Guess secret number: wrong answer

Input(): Guess the secret number: You guessed correct

In this set of input/output, we can see that when we utilize raw_input, we always need to input the proper number While utilizing the input() function, we can even supply the name of a function or variable, and the compiler will assess that.

Here, for instance, the input for input() function has been offered as the name of a function 'secret function()'. The compiler assesses this function call and returns the secret number that we want to discover, and thus, our if condition assesses to be real, although we did not get in the secret number.

Input:

secretfunction()

secret_value

Output:

Raw_input(): Guess secret number: wrong answer

Input(): Guess the secret number: You guessed correct

As described in the very first point, in this example, likewise, we had the ability to just get in the variable name 'secret_number' in the input for 'input()' function, and we had the ability to access the secret worth.

While attempting to call the secret function() in the input for the raw_input() function, it provides us incorrect as the compiler transforms our argument to a string and does not examine it as a function call.

Preventing input vulnerabilities

It is constantly much better to utilize raw_input() in python 2.x and, after that, clearly transform the input to whatever type we need. If we want to take the input of an integer, we can do the following

n = int(raw_input()).

This avoids the harmful calling or examination of functions.

FILTERING

Filtering under one condition

The contrast check in Python is == (double equivalent indication). You ought to double inspect whether you utilized 2 equivalent indications. You may destroy your information if you utilize simply one equivalent indication.

Let's presume that I wish to see if the "Embarked" column amounts to "C." The real variation of the contrast is:

df["Embarked"] == "C"

The output will be:

```
In [38]:  df["Embarked"] == "C"

Out[38]:  258       True
          737       True
          679       True
          88       False
          27       False
          341      False
          438      False
          311       True
          742       True
          118       True
          299       True
          557       True
          700       True
          380       True
          716       True
          527      False
```

If I write the code like this

df["Embarked"] = "C"

It will set all the values as "C" in the Embarked column.

```
In [39]:  df["Embarked"] = "C"

In [40]:  df["Embarked"].head(5)

Out[40]:  258      C
          737      C
          679      C
          88       C
          27       C
          Name: Embarked, dtype: object
```

What if we do not wish to see simply Trues and Falses? What if we wish to see all the info of those whose Embarked is C? To do that:

df[df["Embarked"] == "C"]

Pandas will comprehend that we desire to see those rows that have True worth if we compose it like that. The output is:

Another way to do that might be:

embarked_c_mask = df["Embarked"] == "C"

df[embarked_c_mask]

If we want to filter our data in vice versa:

df[df["Embarked"] != "C"]

It is going to show the rows that their Embarked column is not "C." The output is

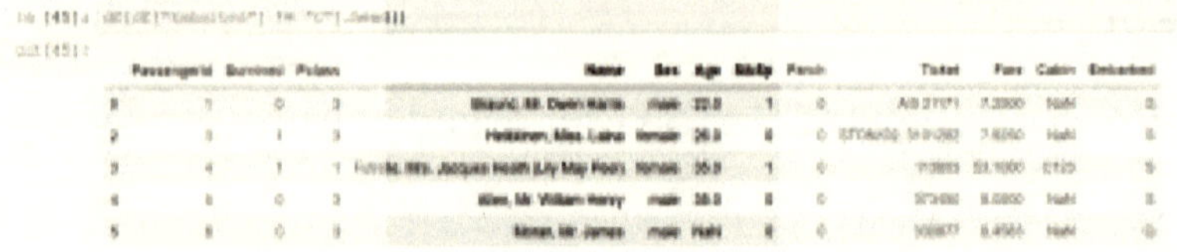

Filtering under two or more condition

AND operator

We are going to utilize AND and OR operators to filter with more than one condition. Let's presume that we wish to see the guests whose Fare is smaller sized than 100 and who are female. We are going to develop 2 brand-new masks to finish that.

df_fare_mask = df["Fare"] < 100

df_sex_mask = df["Sex"] == "female"

df[df_fare_mask & df_sex_mask]

The output is:

OR operator

Let's do another example with OR operator. indication to do that. Let's see the travelers whose fare is more than 500 or older than 70.

df_fare_mask2 = df["Fare"] > 500

df_age_mask = df["Age"] > 70

df[df_fare_mask2 | df_age_mask]

The output is:

Finding the null values with .isnull()

Among the most typical issues in information, science is missing out on worths. To see them, there is a wonderful procedure named null).

With this approach, we can get a boolean series (False or real). As we did previously, by masking the condition, we can draw out the worths which are null.

null_mask = df["Cabin"].isnull()

df[null_mask]

With this code, we are saying that "Show me the passengers whose cabin is unknown." The output is:

```
In [57]: null_mask = df["Cabin"].isnull()
         df[null_mask]
Out[57]:
```

	PassengerId	Survived	Pclass	Name	Sex	Age	SibSp	Parch	Ticket	Fare	Cabin	Embarked
0	1	0	3	Braund, Mr. Owen Harris	male	22.0	1	0	A/5 21171	7.2500	NaN	S
2	3	1	3	Heikkinen, Miss. Laina	female	26.0	0	0	STON/O2. 3101282	7.9250	NaN	S
4	5	0	3	Allen, Mr. William Henry	male	35.0	0	0	373450	8.0500	NaN	S
5	6	0	3	Moran, Mr. James	male	NaN	0	0	330877	8.4583	NaN	Q
7	8	0	3	Palsson, Master. Gosta Leonard	male	2.0	3	1	349909	21.0750	NaN	S
8	9	1	3	Johnson, Mrs. Oscar W (Elisabeth Vilhelmina Berg)	female	27.0	0	2	347742	11.1333	NaN	S
9	10	1	2	Nasser, Mrs. Nicholas (Adele Achem)	female	14.0	1	0	237736	30.0708	NaN	C
12	13	0	3	Saundercock, Mr. William Henry	male	20.0	0	0	A/5. 2151	8.0500	NaN	S
13	14	0	3	Andersson, Mr. Anders Johan	male	39.0	1	5	347082	31.2750	NaN	S
14	15	0	3	Vestrom, Miss. Hulda Amanda Adolfina	female	14.0	0	0	350406	7.8542	NaN	S
15	16	1	2	Hewlett, Mrs. (Mary D Kingcome)	female	55.0	0	0	248706	16.0000	NaN	S
16	17	0	3	Rice, Master. Eugene	male	2.0	4	1	382652	29.1250	NaN	Q

Rather than utilizing this technique on a column, it can be utilized on the entire dataset too. We simply must compose code listed below if we desire to count off the null worths of all columns in a data frame

df.isnull().sum()

Dealing with missing values

There are great deals of dealing methods with missing out on worths; however, in this short article, we are going to utilize "disregard the tuple" and "fill it with average." We are going to overlook the "Cabin" column, given that %70 of that column is missing out on. And we are going to fill the missing out on Ages with a typical worth of that column.

Dropping a column

To drop the "Cabin" column, we must execute the code below.

df.drop(labels = ["Cabin"], axis=1).head()

We used.drop approach to drop the Cabin column. There is a 2 argument above. In the label's argument, we need to define the column names that we wish to drop, in the axis argument, we defined that we drop it column-wise.

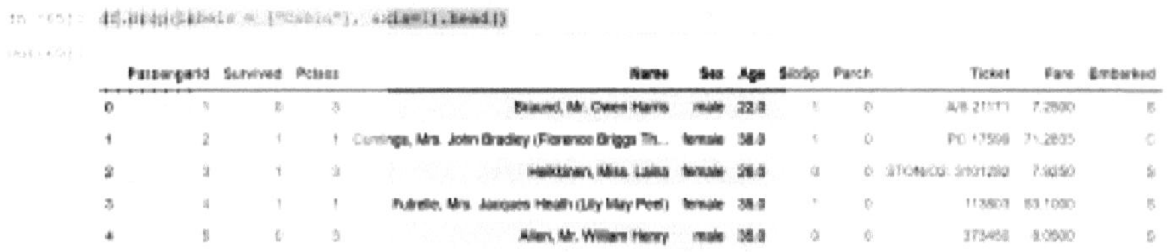

```
In [65]: df.drop(labels = ["Cabin"], axis=1).head()
```

PassengerId	Survived	Pclass	Name	Sex	Age	SibSp	Parch	Ticket	Fare	Embarked
0	1	0	3	Braund, Mr. Owen Harris	male	22.0	1	0	A/5 21171	7.2500	S
1	2	1	1	Cumings, Mrs. John Bradley (Florence Briggs Th...	female	38.0	1	0	PC 17599	71.2835	C
2	3	1	3	Heikkinen, Miss. Laina	female	26.0	0	0	STON/O2. 3101282	7.9250	S
3	4	1	1	Futrelle, Mrs. Jacques Heath (Lily May Peel)	female	35.0	1	0	113803	53.1000	S
4	5	0	3	Allen, Mr. William Henry	male	35.0	0	0	373450	8.0500	S

If you want to drop more than one column, all you must do is add it in the square brackets. For example:

df.drop(labels = ["Cabin", "Name"], axis=1).head()

We are dropping the cabin column and name column at the exact same time. As I pointed out previously, if we understood that we would not utilize these columns, we would have use cols argument of reading_CSV approach to eliminate those columns at the start.

Filling missing values with .fillna()

To fill missing values in a dataframe, there is a method called fill na().

Let's presume that we have great deals of missing out on worths in a column, and we wish to fill them with 0. All we need to do is compose the code listed below

df["columnname"].fillna(0, inplace = True) #with inplace argument, we don't have to write it as

df["columnname"] = df["columnname"].fillna(0, inplace = True)

We can fill it with a specific value too. Let's give an example on Titanic dataset

df["Age"].fillna("Unknown", inplace = True)

Rather of filling with "Unknown" to fill the missing out on worths in the Age column, we are going to utilize the average of that column. To do that:

df['Age'] = df['Age'].fillna((df['Age'].median()))

All we must do is alter the approach at the end if we desire to fill the missing out on worths with mean or something else. After performing this code, we must inspect if there is still null worth in the Age column.

FEW PYTHON PANDAS TIPS TO MAKE DATA ANALYSIS FASTER

1. Styling

Have you ever grumbled about the table output that looks boring when you do head() in Jupyter note pads? Exists a method not to show indexes (particularly when there is currently an ID column)? There're methods to repair these concerns.

A. Highlight all negative values in a dataframe. (example revised from https://pandas.pydata.org/pandas-docs/stable/user_guide/style.html)

```python
import pandas as pd

def color_negative_red(val):

    color = 'red' if val < 0 else 'black'

return 'color: %s' % color

df = pd.DataFrame(dict(col_1=[1.53,-2.5,3.53],

                col_2=[-4.1,5.9,0])
        )

df.style.applymap(color_negative_red)
```

	Col_1	Col_2
0	1.53	-4.1

| 1 | -2.5 | 5.9 |
| 2 | 3.53 | 0 |

B. Hide the index. Try df.head().style.hide_index()!

C. Add hovering effects. (example revised from https://pandas.pydata.org/pandas-docs/stable/reference/api/pandas.io.formats.style.Styler.set_table_styles.html)

df = pd.DataFrame(np.random.randn(5, 3))

df.style.set_table_styles(

[{'selector': 'tr:hover',

  'props': [('background-color', 'yellow')]}]

)

	0	1	2
0	0.995503	0.358578	2.79799
1	0.172723	-1.45818	1.02126
2	0.840297	0.0497946	-1.58906
3	-0.606637	0.923101	1.00091
4	-0.871128	1.20596	-0.980636

D. More CSS styles. You can use CSS to change the appearance of the table.

df = pd.DataFrame(

dict(departure=['SFO', 'SFO', 'LAX', 'LAX', 'JFK', 'SFO'],

    arrival=['ORD', 'DFW', 'DFW', 'ATL', 'ATL', 'ORD'],

```python
        airlines=['Delta','JetBlue','Delta','AA','SouthWest',
                'Delta']),

columns=['airlines', 'departure','arrival'])

df.style.set_table_styles(

[{'selector': 'tr:nth-of-type(odd)',

  'props': [('background', '#eee')]},

{'selector': 'tr:nth-of-type(even)',

  'props': [('background', 'white')]},

{'selector': 'th',

  'props': [('background', '#606060'),

          ('color', 'white'),

          ('font-family', 'verdana')]},

{'selector': 'td',

  'props': [('font-family', 'verdana')]},

]

).hide_index()
```

airlines	departure	arrival
Delta	SFO	ORD
JetBlue	SFO	DFW
Delta	LAX	DFW
AA	LAX	ATL
SouthWest	JFK	ATL
Delta	SFO	ORD

2. Pandas options

You might have experienced this issue while using .head(n) to check the data frame:

(1) There're too many columns / rows in the data frame, and some columns / rows in the middle are omitted.

(2) Columns containing long texts get truncated.

(3) Columns containing floats display too many / too few digits.

One can set

import pandas as pd

pd.options.display.max_columns = 50 # None -> No Restrictions

pd.options.display.max_rows = 200   # None -> Be careful with this

pd.options.display.max_colwidth = 100

pd.options.display.precision = 3

to solve these issues.

3. Group by with multiple aggregations

In SQL we can do aggregations like

SELECT A, B, max(A), avg(A), sum(B), min(B), count(*)

FROM table

GROUP BY A, B

In Pandas it can be done with .groupby() and .agg():

```python
import pandas as pd

import numpy as np

df = pd.DataFrame(dict(A=['coke', 'sprite', 'coke', 'sprite',

                'sprite', 'coke', 'coke'],

             B=['alpha','gamma', 'alpha', 'beta',

               'gamma', 'beta', 'beta'],

             col_1=[1,2,3,4,5,6,7],

             col_2=[1,6,2,4,7,9,3]))

tbl = df.groupby(['A','B']).agg({'col_1': ['max', np.mean],

                'col_2': ['sum','min','count']})

# 'count' will always be the count for number of rows in each group.
```

And the result will look like this:

		col_1		col_2		
		max	mean	sum	min	count
A	**B**					
coke	alpha	3	2.0	3	1	2
	beta	7	6.5	12	3	2
sprite	beta	4	4.0	4	4	1
	gamma	5	3.5	13	6	2

Both the columns and rows are multi-indexed. A fast option to alter it to a dataframe without multi-indices is

tbl = tbl.reset_index()

tbl.columns = ['A', 'B', 'col_1_max', 'col_2_sum', 'col_2_min', 'count']

If you would like to have the column renaming process automated, you can do tbl.columns.get_level_values(0) and tbl.columns.get_level_values(1) to extract the indices in each level and combine them.

4. Column slicing

A few of you may be acquainted with this currently; however, I still discover it beneficial when dealing with a data frame with lots of columns.

df.iloc[:,2:5].head()   # select the 2nd to the 4th column

```
df.loc[:,'column_x':].head()
```

```
# select all columns starting from 'column_x'
```

5. Add row ID / random row ID to each group

To add a row ID / random row ID for each group by A, B, one can first append an ID / random ID to all rows:

```
import numpy as np
```

```
# df: target dataframe
```

```
np.random.seed(0)  # set random seed
```

```
df['random_ID_all'] = np.random.permutation(df.shape[0])
```

```
df['ID_all'] = [i for i in range(1, df.shape[0]+1)]
```

To add a random ID to each group (by A, B), one can then do

```
df['ID'] = df.groupby(['A', 'B'])['ID_all'].rank(method='first', ascending=True).astype(int)
```

```
df['random_ID'] = df.groupby(['A', 'B'])['random_ID_all'].rank(method='first', ascending=True).astype(int)
```

to get

	A	B	ID_all	ID	random_ID_all	random_ID
0	1	2	1	1	7	2
1	1	2	2	2	2	1
2	1	3	3	1	1	1
3	1	3	4	2	4	2
4	1	3	5	3	8	4
5	1	3	6	4	6	3
6	2	4	7	1	3	2
7	2	4	8	2	0	1
8	2	4	9	3	5	3

6. List all unique values in a group

In some cases, after we carried out group by, we 'd like to aggregate the worths in the target column as a list of distinct worths rather of max, minutes, ... and so on. This is how it's done.

```
df = pd.DataFrame(dict(A=['A','A','A','A','A','B','B','B','B'],
                       B=[1,1,1,2,2,1,1,1,2],
                       C=['CA','NY','CA','FL','FL',
                          'WA','FL','NY','WA']))
tbl = df[['A', 'B', 'C']].drop_duplicates()\
```

```
    .groupby(['A','B'])['C']\

    .apply(list)\

    .reset_index()
```

```python
# list to string (separated by commas)
```

```python
tbl['C'] = tbl.apply(lambda x: (','.join([str(s) for s in x['C']])), axis = 1)
```

	A	B	C
0	A	1	CA,NY
1	A	2	FL
2	B	1	WA,FL,NY
3	B	2	WA

Do not forget to alter the separator to anything other than commas if you 'd like to conserve the outcome.

7. Add row total and column total to a numerical dataframe

This is another common data manipulation. All you need is .apply().

```python
df = pd.DataFrame(dict(A=[2,6,3],

                B=[2,2,6],

                C=[3,2,3]))
```

```python
df['col_total']   = df.apply(lambda x: x.sum(), axis=1)
```

```python
df.loc['row_total'] = df.apply(lambda x: x.sum())
```

	A	B	C	col_total
0	2	2	3	7
1	6	2	2	10
2	3	6	3	12
row_total	11	10	8	29

8. Check memory usage

.memory_usage(deep=True) can be utilized on Pandas data-frames to see the quantity of memory utilized (in bytes) for each column. When constructing makers knowing designs that might need a lot of memory in training, it's beneficial.

9. Cumulative sum

From time to time, the cumulative amount is needed when you produce some analytical results. Just do df['cumulative_sum'] = df['target_column'].cumsum().

10. Crosstab

Pd.crosstab() can make your life much easier when you require to count the frequencies for groups formed by 3+ functions.

```python
df = pd.DataFrame(dict(departure=['SFO', 'SFO', 'LAX', 'LAX', 'JFK', 'SFO'],
                       arrival=['ORD', 'DFW', 'DFW', 'ATL', 'ATL', 'ORD'],
                       airlines=['Delta','JetBlue','Delta','AA','SouthWest', 'Delta']))

pd.crosstab(index=[df['departure'], df['airlines']],
            columns=[df['arrival']],
            rownames=['departure', 'airlines'],
            colnames=['arrival'],
            margins=True    # add subtotals
            )
```

departure	arrival airlines	ATL	DFW	ORD	All
JFK	SouthWest	1	0	0	1
LAX	AA	1	0	0	1
	Delta	0	1	0	1
SFO	Delta	0	0	2	2
	JetBlue	0	1	0	1
All		2	2	2	6

FACEBOOK LOGIN USING PYTHON

Python scripting is among the most interesting and appealing things to do, on the other hand, finding out Python. Automation and managing web browser are among them.

In this specific area, we will see how to log in to the Facebook account utilizing Python and the power of selenium.

Selenium automates and manages web browsers, and its activity. We can code in our method to manage internet browser jobs with the assistance of selenium.

We utilize selenium here to open the website of our requirement (in this case, Facebook), and there we examine components throughout the e-mail box, password box, and login button to discover id of them.

Utilizing the find_element_by_id() function offered by the selenium module, we can discover the necessary component (username box, password box, login button).

Utilizing send_keys() function, supplied by the selenium module, we will send out the information into the package.

Setting up 3rd party modules needed

- Selenium
- Getpass

Additional Requirement :

- geckodriver for firefox and
- chrome driver for chrome

Importing necessary modules

Selenium : to automate browser

Time : If we input too quick, to stop briefly running of the script for some seconds as web browsers attempt to discover automation things

Taking username and password as input from the user

Utilizing input() function and passing the timely message as an argument.

Opening a web browser and needed the site

Webdriver.Chrome() will open a brand-new window of chrome. We will wait for things in a variable called chauffeur.

Now utilizing get function, we will open the Facebook site.

Discovering component for sending out and sending out information input

Usage check component tool on the aspect of internet browser of which you desire to discover id. And then, utilize this id integrating with selenium function find_element_by_id() to discover it throughout the web page and conserve it in variables for later usage.

Closing the internet browser

Of the above actions, we must give up the session and will be attained by utilizing driver.quit().

Note: Here driver is the name of the variable you chose for web driver.Chrome().

Complete Code:

```python
from selenium import webdriver

from time import sleep

usr=input('Enter Email Id:')

pwd=input('Enter Password:')


driver = webdriver.Chrome()

driver.get('https://www.facebook.com/')

print ("Opened facebook")

sleep(1)


username_box = driver.find_element_by_id('email')

username_box.send_keys(usr)

print ("Email Id entered")

sleep(1)


password_box = driver.find_element_by_id('pass')

password_box.send_keys(pwd)

print ("Password entered")


login_box = driver.find_element_by_id('loginbutton')

login_box.click()
```

```
print ("Done")

input('Press anything to quit')

driver.quit()

print("Finished")
```

See how such a succinct piece of code can automate things for you.

Freebies:

We can likewise go into the password without showing it on screen for security function. For that, we need to consist of another module called getpass. Now with simply one modification in input declaration of the password, we can input the password without showing it on screen.

```
from getpass import getpass

PWD = getpass('Enter Password:')
```

Getpass triggers the user for a password without echoing. Essentially it lets you go into the password without revealing it on the screen.

You can likewise automate numerous other things like twitter login, tweeting, Facebook logout, and much more.

PROJECT IDEA

Project idea:

The objective of this job is to develop a video game in python in which the user exists with an anagram of a word and needs to think the ideal word within a restricted variety of efforts.

Functions of Project:

The user is provided a set variety of efforts to think the proper word. The variety of efforts depends on the length of the word.

After each inaccurate effort, the user is offered with a tip of the right word.

If the user is not able to think the ideal word within the set number of efforts, the right word is shown, and the video game moves on to the next word.

Ctrl+C or Ctrl+D exits the game.

Implementation:

This tutorial stands just for Linux based systems. This tutorial is composed of a Linux Mint 17.1 system. For carrying out on other Linux systems (Redhat, Arch) see unique note at the end of this tutorial.

In nearly all the Linux based systems there is a file situated at directory site area "/ usr/share/dict/" under various names like "cracklib-small"(Ubuntu-based systems)," words"(Redhat, Arch) which consists of words from dictionary and are typically utilized by lots of applications to execute functions such as "spell-check."

In this task, I will be utilizing the exact same file to develop a video game of anagrams.

Checking out the file can offer us all the words needed for the video game. The words in the file are separated with a new-line, so while checking out the file, we require to divide the words based upon the new-line character to get private words.

The code for the exact same would appear like:

loc='/usr/share/dict/cracklib-small'

with open(loc) as f:

content=f.read().split('\n')

f.close()

The file likewise consists of words like "zoo's"; however, we do not desire such words in our video game so we can omit them. To prevent making the video game too basic, I chose to likewise omit words of length less than 5; however, this action is optional and can be avoided.

The code for the very same appear as:

l=len(content)

words=[]

for i in range(0,l):

    if'\" in content[i] or len(content[i])<5:

```
    continue
```

```
words.append(content[i])
```

The file likewise includes words like "2nd,3rd" at the start of the file. To avoid them from appearing in our video game, we omit them by:

```
words=words[1:]
```

```
d=len(words)
```

```
words=words[:d]
```

"words" include all the words we require for the video game to continue.

We can pick a word for a specific round of the video game by:

```
word=words[random.randint(0,d)]
```

The word would be arbitrarily selected from the list of words developed.

To produce the anagram of the word, we require to shuffle the characters. This can be done by:

```
shuffle=list(word)
```

```
random.shuffle(shuffle)
```

, if the length of the word selected for the round is more than 7, the user gets 7 efforts else the number of efforts is 5.

```
if len(word)>7:
    chances=7
```

```
else:
    chances=5
    tries=0
```

The variable "shots" keeps an eye on the variety of efforts taken by the user. We initialize it to absolutely no.

Throughout each user effort, we take their input and compare it with the appropriate word; if they match, we praise the user and provide the next anagram else we supply them with a tip.

To produce tip for a specific word, we pick 2 random integers in between 0 and the length of the word.

```
t1=random.randint(0,len(word))
```

```
t2=random.randint(0,len(word))
```

We show the proper characters at these 2 positions t1 and t2, and at all the other positions, we show “.”.

```
hint=""
for i in range(0,len(word)):
    if i==t1 or i==t2:
        hint=hint+word[i]
    else:
        hint=hint+"."
print hint
```

We show the correct word, and the video game continues if the number of attempts= number of possibilities.

```
if tries==chances:
    print "The answer was "+word
```

Unique Note: To make the code as platform independent as possible, we can select the area of the file dynamically utilizing the platform module of python.

```
os=platform.dist()[0]

if os=='LinuxMint' or os=='Ubuntu':

    loc='/usr/share/dict/cracklib-small'

else:

    loc='/usr/share/dict/words'
```

Software Tools Required: The game can be implemented in Python using modules platform and random.

Github Link: https://github.com/sub123/practice/blob/master/python/anagramwa.py

TEXT ANALYSIS IN PYTHON 3

Book's / Document's Content Analysis

Patterns within the composed text are not the exact same throughout all authors or languages. This enables linguists to study the language of origin or prospective authorship of texts where these qualities are not straight understood, such as the Federalist Papers of the American Revolution.

Goal: In this case research study, we will analyze the homes of private books in a book collection from numerous authors and numerous languages. More particularly, we will look at book lengths, a variety of distinct words, and how these qualities cluster by the language of or authorship.

Source: Project Gutenberg is the earliest virtual library of books. It intends to digitize and archive cultural works, and at present, consists of over 50,000 books, all formerly released and now readily available digitally. Download a few of these English & French books and the Portuguese & German books too for analysis. Put all these books together in a folder called Books with subfolders English, French, German & Portuguese.

Word Frequency in Text

We are going to construct a function that will count the word frequency in a text. We will think about a sample test text, & later, we will change the sample text with the text file of books that we have simply downloaded.

```
text="This is my test text. We're keeping this text brief to keep things workable."

text = text.lower()
```

Word frequency can be counted in numerous ways. We are going to code, 2 such methods (simply for understanding). One is utilizing for loop and the other utilizing Counter from collections, which shows to be faster than the previous one. The function will return a dictionary of distinct words & its frequency as a key-value pair. So, we code:

```
from collections import Counter
```

```
def count_words(text):                #counts word frequency
        skips = [".", ", ", ":", ";", "'", '"']
        for ch in skips:
        text = text.replace(ch, "")
        word_counts = {}
        for word in text.split(" "):
        if word in word_counts:
        word_counts[word]+= 1
        else:
        word_counts[word]= 1
        return word_counts

        # >>>count_words(text) You can check the function
```

```python
def count_words_fast(text):         #counts word frequency
using Counter from collections

    text = text.lower()

    skips = [".", ",", ":", ";", "'", '"']

    for ch in skips:

    text = text.replace(ch, "")

    word_counts = Counter(text.split(" "))

    return word_counts


    # >>>count_words_fast(text) You can check the function
```

Output : The output is a dictionary holding the unique words of the sample text as key and the frequency of each word as value. Comparing the output of both the functions, we have:

{'were': 1, 'is': 1, 'manageable': 1, 'to': 1, 'things': 1, 'keeping': 1, 'my': 1, 'test': 1, 'text': 2, 'keep': 1, 'short': 1, 'this': 2}

Counter({'text': 2, 'this': 2, 'were': 1, 'is': 1, 'manageable': 1, 'to': 1, 'things': 1, 'keeping': 1, 'my': 1, 'test': 1, 'keep': 1, 'short': 1})

Checking Out Books into Python: Since we achieved success in evaluating our word frequency works with the sample text. Now, we are going to test the functions with the books, which we downloaded as a text file.

We are going to develop a function called read_book() which will read our books in Python and wait as a long string in a variable and return it. The specification of the function will be the place of the book.txt to be checked out and will be passed while calling the function.

```python
def read_book(title_path): #read a book and return it as a string

    with open(title_path, "r", encoding ="utf8") as current_file:

    text = current_file.read()

    text = text.replace("\n", "").replace("\r", "")

    return text
```

Overall Unique words: We are going to develop another function called word_stats(), which will take the word frequency dictionary(output of count_words_fast()/ count_words()) as a parameter. The function will return the overall no of special words(sum/total type in the word frequency dictionary) and a dict_values holding overall count of them together, as a tuple.

```python
def word_stats(word_counts):        # word_counts = count_words_fast(text)

    num_unique = len(word_counts)

    counts = word_counts.values()

    return (num_unique, counts)
```

Calling the functions: So, finally, we are going to check out a book, for example-- English variation of Romeo and Juliet, and gather details on word frequency, special words, the overall count of special words, etc. from the functions.

```python
text = read_book("./Books / English / Shakespeare / Romeo and Juliet.txt")

word_counts = count_words_fast(text)

(num_unique, counts) = word_stats(word_counts)

print(num_unique, sum(counts))
```

Output: 5118 40776

With the assistance of the functions that we developed, we familiarized that there are 5118 distinct words in the English variation of Romeo and Juliet, and The Sum of the frequency of the distinct words summarize to 40776. We can understand which word took place one of the most in the book & can have fun with various variations of books of various languages to learn about them and their statistics with the assistance of the above functions.

Plotting Characteristic Features of Books

We are going to plot (i) Book-length Vs. The number of Unique words for all the books of various languages utilizing matplotlib. We will import pandas to develop a pandas dataframe, which will hold details on books as columns. We will classify these columns by various classifications such as-- "language", "author", "title", "length" & "special". To outline book-length along x-axis and Number of special words along y-axis, we code:

```
import os

import pandas as pd

book_dir = "./Books"

os.listdir(book_dir)


stats = pd.DataFrame(columns =("language", "author", "title", "length", "unique"))

# check > > >stats

title_num = 1

for language in os.listdir(book_dir):
```

```python
    for author in os.listdir(book_dir+"/"+language):

    for title in os.listdir(book_dir+"/"+language+"/"+author):

    inputfile = book_dir+"/"+language+"/"+author+"/"+title

    print(inputfile)

    text = read_book(inputfile)

    (num_unique, counts) = word_stats(count_words_fast(
text))

    stats.loc[title_num]=      language,      author.capitalize(),
title.replace(".txt", ""),

    sum(counts), num_unique

    title_num+= 1

import matplotlib.pyplot as plt

plt.plot(stats.length, stats.unique, "bo-")


plt.loglog(stats.length, stats.unique, "ro")


stats[stats.language =="English"] #to check information on eng-
lish books

plt.figure(figsize =(10, 10))

subset = stats[stats.language =="English"]

plt.loglog(subset.length, subset.unique, "o", label ="English",
color ="crimson")

subset = stats[stats.language =="French"]

plt.loglog(subset.length, subset.unique, "o", label ="French",
color ="forestgreen")
```

```python
subset = stats[stats.language =="German"]

plt.loglog(subset.length, subset.unique, "o", label ="German",
color ="orange")

subset = stats[stats.language =="Portuguese"]

plt.loglog(subset.length, subset.unique, "o", label ="Portuguese",
color ="blueviolet")

plt.legend()

plt.xlabel("Book Length")

plt.ylabel("Number of Unique words")

plt.savefig("fig.pdf")

plt.show()
```

Output: We outlined 2 charts, the very first one representing every book of various language & author as just a book. The red dots in the very first chart represent a single book, and they are linked by blue lines., signing up with the points.

These charts assist in analyzing truths aesthetically about various books of brilliant origin. From the chart, we familiarized that Portuguese books are longer in length and have a higher number of special words than English or German books. Outlining such information shows to be of fantastic aid for linguists.

CONCLUSION

Python is a vital aspect of the toolkit of the knowledge specialist, as it is specially built to make repetitive research and information adaptation, and anybody who has treated vast amounts of information obviously understands how much it is replicated. The intelligence experts provide a method to cope with dirty work and are parallel to the more rewarding and interesting aspects of the job.

Data specialists will always note the number of other Python resources that are readily accessible. Such libraries like Numby, Pandas, and Matplotlib allow the knowledge specialist to execute his functions and you can look at the basics of Python

BOOKS IN THIS SERIES

Get Your Website Ranked Higher

The eBook series, "Get Your Website Ranked Higher" will provide the reader with user friendly resources and guides focused on top programming languages and essential information beginner web developers use to create high ranking websites. Use the eBooks in this series to learn the basic programming languages and insights to start your journey as web developer with the goal of building your own custom website. These guides are not meant to be an exhaustive reference to everything on each subject. This resource is simply meant to be a starting point for beginners that is easy to digest and follow.

Get Your Website Ranked Higher: Simplified Roadmap For Javascript Beginners - Stop Wasting Time And Start Learning The Essentials! What You Need To Know Before You Start Working On Your Website

Have you just started building your first website or app? Are you an entrepreneur or small business owner looking to increase sales and get your website ranked higher? Is front-end web development a hobby or are you just starting? Missing out on sales or need to build your brand online? Are you confused, stuck, or feeling information overload? If you answered yes, continue reading.

I personally started working to building a website for my business and struggled to get the results I wanted. Even with website templates I still had to edit the content and adapt the template to

suit my individual's needs. I still had to have a fundamental understanding of coding languages. As I tried to build a website tailored to my needs I was constantly getting hung up on small details and It would cost me a lot of time, frustration, and eventually money. When I would search for answers I would get overwhelmed by endless information and often would be left more confused than when I started. It soon became clear I needed a condensed, organized, roadmap to help learn the essentials of JavaScript and how it's used without unnecessary information bogging down my learning curve. I adjusted my search to seek out the essentials and again was overwhelmed by all the information. Determined there was a better way, I found myself seeking out experienced web developers to provide focused content I could use as resource to help me learn. This simple idea snowballed and soon I hired a web developer to help create this eBook to focus on content to help others jump start their learning curve.

If you don't capitalize on this condensed learning material you could find yourself continuing to be frustrated, confused, and missing opportunities. Below is what you can expect.

You'll find the content is designed to help you easily learn the essentials of JavaScript. You will be armed and ready to learn more complicated JavaScript libraries and frameworks to maximize your websites impact and get it ranked higher. As you work through the content you will be well versed in JavaScript and will overcome common mistakes. Soon you'll be prepared to navigate more complicated coding. You will have the necessary foundation to build your website or modify it to suit your needs. Ultimately, the goal is to prepare you for your journey into mastering JavaScript basics.

When you begin to read you quickly find this is no-nonsense guide. It is organized to help you understand and learn the basics of JavaScript coding language. The content builds on itself and provides a clear path to learn the pertinent information. The content is distilled down to save time and energy. Also, it offers the experienced developer insight into the history of web development, how different technologies interact and work together,

and resources to expand their capabilities. This powerful tool will help you build out your digital portfolio and grow as a developer. Reference this condensed guide for answers to commonly asked questions anywhere you have internet. This guide is not meant to be an exhaustive reference to everything JavaScript. This resource is simply meant to be a starting point for beginners that is easy to digest and follow.

This foundation in coding language can provide job safety, repeatable success, constantly evolving coding skills, and help you on your journey to make new products and services. As it stands now, taking time learning these skills is your best low risk high reward investment across the board. I challenge you to take the information provided to you in this book and get your website ranked higher.

Remember, if we continue to learn we continue to grow. Never stop learning!

Do Not Go Yet; One Last Thing to Do
I would be very happy if you would give a short review
of Amazon if you liked the book or found it useful. Your
encouragement really makes a difference, and I personally
read all reviews to get your input and develop the book.

Thank you for your help again!

www.ingramcontent.com/pod-product-compliance
Lightning Source LLC
Chambersburg PA
CBHW020734160726
47993CB00006B/2452